KARATE HANDBOOK

KARATE HANDBOOK

J. Allen Queen

Sterling Publishing Co., Inc.   New York

To my son, Alex

Edited by Robert Hernandez

Library of Congress Cataloging-in-Publication Data

Queen, J. Allen.
  Karate handbook.

  Includes index.
  Summary: Instructions in basic techniques of karate especially for the
young child, with more than 200 photographs.
  1. Karate for children–Juvenile literature.
[1. Karate] I. Jones, Samuel, ill. II. Title.
GV1114.32.Q44   1986   796.8'153   85-28096
ISBN 0-8069-6286-0
ISBN 0-8069-6287-9 (lib. bdg.)
ISBN 0-8069-6288-7 (pbk.)

First Paperback Printing, 1987

CONTENTS

Acknowledgments

I would like to express my sincere appreciation to the following students who have devoted several years of their youth to the art and sport of karate, in addition to their assistance in making this book a reality: Antwaine Brown, William Burns, Kristi Clary, Jimmy Davis, Nikki Dixon, Jason Fall, Andy Ford, Lora Goins, Bobby Knott, Jarius Laughter, Jonathan Lovelace, Heather McDowell, Oscar Ortago, Andriana Ortega, Ginger Philbeck, Ronald Philbeck, Andrew Phillips, Michael Phillips, Max Washington, Je'Myrianee Weaver, Ernest Wilson, Robert Wingo, and to all of the students of North Elementary School in Kings Mountain, North Carolina.

Thanks to Judy Herndon, for drawing the illustrations, and to Samuel Jones, III, for the photography.

Additionally, I would like to acknowledge my sensei, Master Carl Smith, III, for his many years of karate instruction, and to Mr. Carl Clary for his assistance.

1

QUESTIONS ABOUT KARATE

Welcome to the exciting world of karate. By learning the basic techniques of this sport, you can begin to earn higher grades in school, gain self-confidence, and be able to defend yourself against any attacker. Let's begin by looking at the six most often asked questions about karate.

Why Karate?

Unlike many team sports, karate gives you the chance to use your physical skills for self-defense. Karate is a sport in which you can enter contests to win awards. Also the movements that you learn to do with your body are beautiful and fun. You can practice karate by yourself, with a partner, or in a group.

What Is Karate?

Karate began in the Orient over two thousand years ago. It has now become popular all over the world. To do karate, you combine leg, arm, and body movements for self defense. You don't actually hit anyone when you practice karate. You learn to stop your punches and kicks before you touch your partner's body. You would only hit a person if he or she attacks you or tries to hurt you.

Illus. 1. These girls prepare themselves for karate practice.

Can the Practice of Karate Help My Development?

Your body and mind are always changing as you grow. You learn that you need friends, family, and fun recreation to be happy. Your personality develops during this period in your life. Your schoolwork, friends, and after-school activities all influence you. It's important to be as good as you can be in these activities. Most teachers agree that a sport or hobby which lets you think and plan as you move arms, legs, and body at the same time is good for you. What's more, karate is fun.

What Can I Gain from Karate Training?

As you learn karate, you will become more self-confident and more independent. You will enjoy doing things for yourself. In addition to improved physical fitness,

Illus. 2. You can do karate by yourself or in a group.

Illus. 3. Your balance will improve as you practice karate.

you will be able to think better in school and recreational activities. If you practice karate for six months or longer, your school grades can improve. You may also notice that you become more helpful around your home. You learn self-discipline to control your anger and fear.

Could You Give Some Examples of Students Who Gained from Karate?

Ben, seven years old, was shy and quiet before learning karate. His teacher said that his classmates picked on him. After about five months of training, Ben's be-

havior began to change. He became more self-confident. Although Ben never had to use karate to defend himself, he gained the respect of his classmates.

Aaron, a fifth-grader, was clumsy and small for his age. His parents enrolled him in a karate class. After two months, Aaron began to improve. His progress was slow at first, but after eight months Aaron had grown stronger and became less clumsy. Aaron's grades greatly improved within the first year.

Kim, ten years old, had a hard time with her schoolwork and getting along with her friends. She refused to clean her room or do any chores at home. After starting karate, Kim's behavior improved immediately. She received more attention from her friends and classmates because of her karate ability. And Kim soon got along better with her friends. She did chores at home and kept her room very clean. After a year of karate study, she had learned to improve on her own and enjoyed the feeling of success.

What Is the Best Way to Pick a Karate School?

Unfortunately, many karate instructors will not accept you into their classes if you are under ten years old. But even worse, some instructors will not give you good individual guidance.

Although an instructor may be excellent for adults, he may not know how to teach you in the best way. Young people need more time to learn each karate skill. You cannot master some karate skills because of your size and age. The instructor may not explain things clearly to you like your teacher at school. And he may not have the patience to teach you a new karate skill. The ideal teacher should have an advanced ranking in karate (first-degree black belt or higher). He should also have experience as a schoolteacher and a real interest in young children. If your karate teacher has these qualities, you will have a better chance to learn properly.

Illus. 5. This girl gets individual instruction from her teacher.

This book will give you the basic knowledge in karate. Only a good instructor can teach you the more advanced levels correctly. Once you have learned the basics, you will need to find a karate instructor to show you the advanced skills. Rememer the following three points:

1. *Find a helpful and patient instructor.* Don't get one who screams or hits his students when they make mistakes. You learn from your mistakes. And you're going to make plenty at the beginning. You need someone who won't yell or make you nervous.

2. *Take a class with people of your age.* You will get confused learning karate with grown-ups. Adults are bigger and their muscles are stronger and better developed than yours. Adult classes move too quickly for young people.

3. *Promotion to the next rank should be based on your ability.* Many instructors promote students on their success in a karate tournament. You should be judged on your ability and not whether or not you win a tournament. In fact, many students never enter them. Some of the greatest karate men and women in history were never even in a tournament.

Illus. 6. It is important to have a teacher who really cares about you.

2
GETTING STARTED

Now that you have a better idea of what karate can do for you, it's time to begin. This chapter looks at the clothing and equipment used in karate. Then you can practice the exercises described here to stretch and warm up your muscles. This is very important to do before you practice karate. It keeps you flexible.

KARATE UNIFORM

The clothing that you wear when you do karate is usually a jacket and pants. It is often white, but it can be any color. The traditional uniform is called a "gi" (pronounced *gee*).

Karate suits are excellent for practice. But you can also wear loose pants and a sweat shirt at home. You will need a gi when you join a class. Order one from your instructor or from a karate magazine.

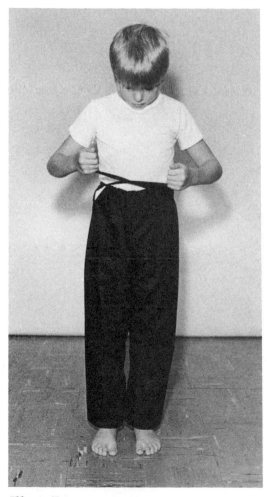

Illus. 7.

Illus. 8.

Draw the traditional-style pants tight around your waist with the drawstrings (Illus. 7). Newer-style pants have snaps, zippers, or buttons. Then put on the jacket (Illus. 8).

There are four major colors of belts that show a person's rank in karate: white for beginners, green for intermediates, brown for advanced levels, and black for experts. Some instructors use additional colors to show ranks between the four major belts. (See Chapter 5 for more details about the other belts and ranks.)

Always wear your belt around your waist when you do karate. Use the following six steps to tie your belt correctly:

Illus. 9. Step 1: Fold the belt in half in front of you to find the middle. Hold the two ends in your left hand and the folded middle in your right.

Illus. 10. Step 2: Open the belt and line up the middle of it across your waist.

Illus. 11. Step 3: Wrap both ends behind your back and bring them around to the front again.

Illus. 12. Step 4: Pull the left end up between your jacket and belt at your waist.

Illus. 13. Step 5: Cross the right end over and then under the left end.

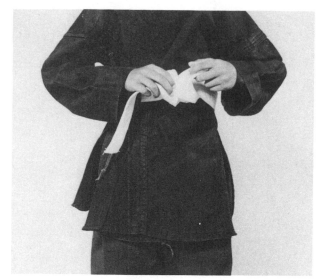

Illus. 14a.

Illus. 14 and 14a. Step 6: Tie the belt tightly into a knot and let the two ends fall in front of your gi.

Illus. 15. When tied correctly, both ends of the belt are the same length.

You don't need much equipment to start. In fact, few items are required. You can practice in any large room, garage, or open space. In most karate classes, punching bags, mirrors, weights, and gloves are available for use. You should purchase your own mouthpiece, and don't let anyone else use it.

Illus. 16. A mouthpiece protects your teeth and gums.

Illus. 17. As you increase in rank, you should buy your own hand and foot gloves. They form to the shape of your hands and feet and give extra protection when you spar with another person. Boys should wear a cup athletic supporter in case they get hit accidentally in the groin area. It can be purchased at most pharmacies.

KARATE RULES

A karate school is called a "dojo" (pronounced *doe-joe*). Rules are different from school to school. But all require you to do the traditional bow when greeting an instructor or higher-ranking student. You also bow when entering or leaving the dojo or area of practice. The bow shows respect to your instructor, classmates, and opponents in a tournament. You should bow when you begin or end a karate exercise with a partner.

You must treat your instructor with respect in class. Most instructors don't allow you to talk without permission. In addition, noisy disruptions are not allowed in class. Fighting, other than for self-defense, is forbidden. You must learn and practice discipline and self-control.

Classes are usually offered two or three times per week. It is important for you

Illus. 18. To bow, hold your hands in front and look straight ahead.

Illus. 19. Bend forward slightly, keeping your eyes on the person. Then stand straight.

Illus. 20. Students and their instructor bow during a class.

to practice every day at home or in the dojo. Here is one golden rule: It is better to practice daily for shorter periods of time than to practice once a week for longer periods.

WARM-UP EXERCISES

Get into a habit of exercising before karate practice. Your muscles can be easily hurt without proper warm-up exercises. Do the basic movements described in this section to warm up your body. Stretching is the most important activity. It makes you more flexible.

As you do these exercises, begin slowly. Gradually increase your movement. Exercise should never be painful. It is a good idea for you to have a checkup by your doctor before beginning any exercise program. This is especially true if you are overweight or if you have a special problem.

Illus. 21.

Illus. 22.

Illus. 23.

Neck Roll

This exercise loosens your neck and strengthens the muscles. Repeat it five times to each side. Increase with practice.

Illus. 21. Stand with your feet shoulder-width apart and turn your head to the left.

Illus. 22. Roll your head rearwards.

Illus. 23. Then roll your head to the right. Return to a straight position.

Illus. 24.

Illus. 25.

Illus. 26.

Arm Rotation

This exercise loosens your shoulders and arms. Repeat it ten times with each arm.

Illus. 24. Stand straight with your feet shoulder-width apart and swing your right arm forward.

Illus. 25. Then swing your arm up-wards.

Illus. 26. Now swing it behind you like you are winding a large clock. Finish with your arm at your side.

Body Twist

This stretches the muscles of your upper body. Begin slowly with the first four twists. Increase the speed and force with your last six moves for each side.

Illus. 27. Extend your arms in front, then twist to your left.

Illus. 28. Now swing to your right and return to the front.

Leg Swing

The leg swing loosens your legs and improves your balance. Repeat it five times for each leg. Increase the height with each repetition.

Illus. 29. Take a large step rearwards with your right leg.

Illus. 30. Lift your right leg forward. Raise it to waist level and lower it.

Leg Stretch

Do leg stretches to loosen your leg muscles and to become more flexible. Repeat the exercise ten times with each leg. Try harder with each time.

Illus. 31. Sit on the floor with your left leg folded behind you.

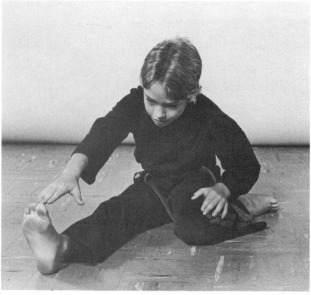

Illus. 32. Bend forward and try to touch the toes of your right leg.

Body Bend

This exercise stretches the leg muscles and makes you more flexible at the waist. Repeat it five times.

Illus. 33. Sit on the floor. Bend forward with your legs straight.

Illus. 34. Grasp your ankles as you bend forward. Hold for two seconds.

27

Split

Splits help to make you flexible. They also increase the height, power, and speed of your kicks. Be careful not to strain the muscles of your inner thigh. It may seem

Illus. 35. Spread your legs as far apart as possible.

Illus. 36. Turn your left foot and head to the left for a side split.

uncomfortable at first. You should feel tightness, but *don't* push until it becomes painful. Repeat it for each leg. *Caution: Do This Exercise Slowly.*

Illus. 37. Slowly stretch your body down to the floor.

Illus. 38. Carefully stretch until you can't go any further. Use your hands for support. *Don't stretch too hard.*

Illus. 39. This girl does a full split, which is very difficult for boys to do. *Do not* try this unless you have had a lot of practice with an instructor.

3
BASIC TECHNIQUES

STANCES

A strong stance is the most important part of karate. It is your solid foundation. You are only as strong as your stance. You begin all karate movements from a stance.

Face forward in the direction of the stance. Keep your shoulders and back straight. Tighten the muscles in your stomach and hips. Place your hands in front or at your sides as you wish.

The main stances (front and side views) are shown in the photographs. The foot positions are shown in the drawings.

Closed Stance

Use the closed stance with your feet together to do the traditional bow. Place your weight equally on both feet.

Illus. 40. Front view.

Illus. 41. Side view.

Illus. 42. Foot position.

Ready Stance

The ready is also known as the open or set stance. Use it to begin most karate exercises and after you complete them. Place your weight equally on both feet, which are shoulder-width apart.

Illus. 43. Front view. Illus. 44. Side view.

Illus. 45. Foot position.

Front Stance

The front stance lets you move to the front or to the rear. It is one of the strongest and most flexible stances in karate. Keep your back leg straight with your knee locked. In the left front stance (Illus. 46), place your left leg in front. Bend at the knee and keep a little more than half your body weight on it. Do the opposite for the right front stance.

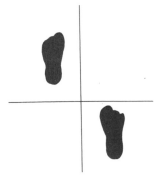

Illus. 46. Front view. Illus. 47. Side view. Illus. 48. Foot position.

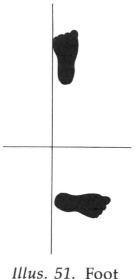

Illus. 49. Front view. *Illus. 50.* Side view.

Illus. 51. Foot position.

Back Stance

One of the most all-around stances is the back stance. In the right back stance (Illus. 49), put three-quarters of your body weight on your right back leg. Put the rest of your weight on your front leg. Do the opposite for the left back stance. Bend both knees slightly. Your feet should form an L-shape.

Cat Stance

The cat stance makes you look like a cat crouching and preparing to strike. With most of your body weight on your back leg, your front leg is free to strike quickly. Shift all of your weight to your back leg when you kick with your front leg. In a right cat stance (Illus. 52), your right leg is the back leg. Do the opposite for the left cat stance (Illus. 54).

Illus. 52. Right cat stance.

Illus. 54. Left cat stance.

Illus. 55. Foot position (left cat stance).

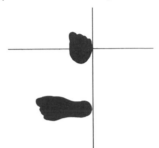

Horse Stance

The horse stance makes you look like you are riding a horse. Spread your feet two shoulder-widths apart and bend your knees deeply. Place your body weight equally on both legs and feet. Keep your back straight. This stance may be difficult for you to do at first. Practice it until it seems easier. In the horse stance, you can use different blocks or attack an opponent with many types of strikes or kicks. It is harder for an opponent to hit you when you are in the horse stance.

Illus. 56. Foot position.

Illus. 57. Front view.

PUNCHES

When you do a karate punch, you must close your fist correctly. Follow these three steps:

Illus. 58. Step 1: *Close* your fingers tightly at the second knuckle.

Illus. 59. Step 2: *Roll* your fingers into the palm of your hand.

Illus. 60. Step 3: *Press* your thumb over your index and middle fingers.

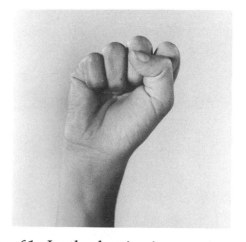

Illus. 61. In the beginning, you can remember how to make a fist by using the first word of each step: *close, roll,* and *press.* Soon you will be able to close your fist correctly without thinking about it.

Illus. 62.

Illus. 63.

Illus. 64.

Forward Fist

Illus. 62. Stand in a ready stance with your right fist held palm upwards at your hip. Hold your left hand in front with your palm held downwards.

Illus. 63. Punch in a straight line, turning your fist until the palm faces downwards.

Illus. 64. At the same time, pull back your left hand and turn it palm upwards into a fist at your hip. The first two knuckles of your index and middle fingers are the first to hit the target.

Illus. 65.

Illus. 66.

Back Fist

Illus. 65. Stand in a horse stance with your right arm held parallel to the floor in front of your chest. Keep your left fist at your hip.

Illus. 66. Snap your arm out to the side, extending your elbow. Then return your fist back in front of your chest.

Illus. 67. Punch with the knuckles of your index and middle fingers.

Illus. 67.

Knife-Hand Strike

Illus. 68. Stand in a back stance (or horse or cat stance) with your open left hand held under your right ear. Cross your right arm in front.

Illus. 69. Strike downwards with your left hand while turning your hips to the left. At the same time, pull your left hand back towards your hip.

Illus. 70. Keep your striking hand open with your thumb bent towards the palm. Strike with the outer edge of your hand (the shaded area in the drawing).

Illus. 68.

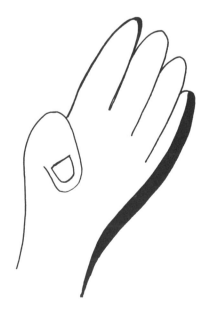

Illus. 69.

Illus. 70.

KICKS

Kicks are your strongest weapons in karate since your leg muscles are larger and stronger than your arm muscles. But kicks are slower and less accurate than punches. When you kick, you are supported by one leg. You must learn to shift your body weight to improve your balance.

The front, side, and roundhouse kicks are introduced in this chapter. (See Chapter 6 for more advanced kicks: the crescent, spin, fake front roundhouse, and hook kicks.) It is important to master the basic kicks first.

Illus. 71. Good balance is the secret to kicking effectively.

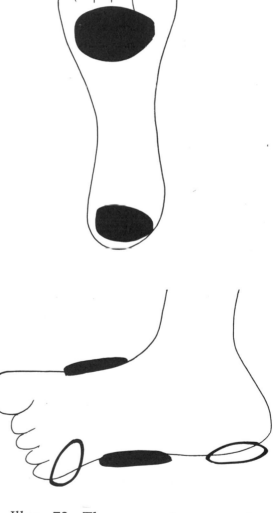

Illus. 72. There are six areas of the foot used for striking: ball, heel, top, outside and inside edges, and bottom.

Illus. 73.

Illus. 74.

Illus. 75.

Front Kick

This kick is done with a snapping action of your lower leg. Use the following steps to do a right front kick:

Illus. 73. Stand in a left front stance.

Illus. 74. Raise your right knee to waist level. Pull back with your right foot and raise your toes for the kick.

Illus. 75. Snap your lower leg forward, locking your knee as you kick. Then snap your right foot back towards your left knee. Return your foot to its original position. Do the opposite for a left front kick.

42

Illus. 76.

Illus. 77.

Illus. 78.

Side Kick

You can do a side kick low, medium, or high. Begin by kicking low and increase your height as you become more flexible. Follow these steps to do a left side kick:

Illus. 76. Stand in a horse stance.

Illus. 77. Lift your left leg so that your foot is about as high as your right knee as shown.

Illus. 78. Shift your body to the far right as you raise your knee higher. Kick your left leg to the side, using the bottom of your foot to strike the target. Return your left foot above your right knee. Return to a horse stance. Do the opposite for a right side kick.

Roundhouse Kick

This is a powerful kick to aim at an opponent's stomach, chest, or head. Your body weight is shifted and your balance is very important. Do the following steps for a right roundhouse kick:

Illus. 79. Begin from a right back stance.

Illus. 80. Raise your right leg behind your right hip and balance on your left leg. Turn your left knee a little outward.

Illus. 81.

Illus. 82.

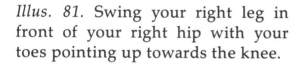

Illus. 81. Swing your right leg in front of your right hip with your toes pointing up towards the knee.

Illus. 82. Continue the circular motion to the left as you kick your right leg and foot.

Illus. 83. Strike your target with the ball of your right foot. Return your right foot and leg behind your right hip. Get into your original back stance. Do the opposite for a left roundhouse kick.

Illus. 83.

BLOCKS

Punches, strikes and kicks can be used in offense or defense. Blocks are just for defense. You deflect your opponent's attack. Blocks can be made low, medium, high, inside, or outside.

Low Block

Use the low block to defend against an attack to your stomach or groin area. In a front stance, you can use a low block to deflect a strike or kick to your body. Either hand can be used to block. Follow these steps to do a right low block:

Illus. 84. Stand in a right forward stance. Raise your right fist to the left side of your head. Extend your left hand straight in front of you in a ready position, palm down.

Illus. 85. Bring your right arm downwards and across your chest.

Illus. 86.

Illus. 86. At the same time, pull back your left hand to your waist, palm up. Notice that your right hand is in front and your right leg is forward.

High Block

Use the high block to protect your head and face. The same hand and leg are in front for the high block.

Get into a right front stance to do a right high block:

Illus. 87. Place your left hand in front and across your chest. Your right fist is at your right hip.

Illus. 88. Bring your right arm up across your chest, palm down.

Illus. 87.

Illus. 88.

Illus. 89.

Illus. 90.

Illus. 89. Turn your right arm so your palm faces forward and continue lifting it above your head.

Illus. 90. At the same time, pull back your left fist to your left hip in a ready position. Do the opposite for a left high block.

Inside Middle Block

The inside middle block protects your upper body area. Your blocking arm is brought inside and across. Follow these steps to do an inside middle block with your left arm:

Illus. 91. In a ready stance, place your right arm across your chest. Your left fist is at your left hip.

Illus. 91.

Illus. 92.

Illus. 93.

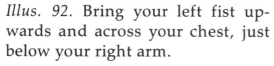

Illus. 92. Bring your left fist upwards and across your chest, just below your right arm.

Illus. 93. Turn your left forearm to the left side. Block with the upper portion of your left forearm.

Illus. 94. Pull back your right fist alongside your right hip, palm up. Do the opposite for an inside middle block with your right arm.

Illus. 94.

Illus. 95.

Illus. 96.

Illus. 97.

Outside Middle Block

The outside middle block protects your middle or upper body area. From either a front or back stance, use these steps to do an outside middle block with your left fist:

Illus. 95. In a right back stance, shift your hips a little to the left as you bring your left fist to the side.

Illus. 96. Swing your left arm inward with your palm towards your face as you turn your body to the right.

Illus. 97. Continue swinging your left arm until it reaches the middle of your body to block the strike. At the same time, pull back your right fist.

COMBINATION MOVEMENTS

Now it's time to make your karate practice fun and useful. You have been introduced to the basic stances, punches, strikes, kicks, and blocks. With some thought and coordination, you can combine these moves to defend yourself against an attack. It also shows you how to really get into the action.

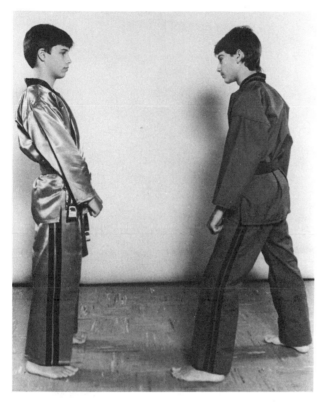

Sequence 1

Illus. 98. Face your partner in a ready stance (far left). He stands in a left front stance.

Illus. 99. He brings a hammer blow downward to your head.

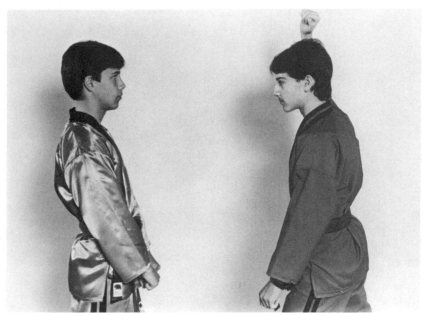

Illus. 100. To defend yourself, shift into a left front stance. Stop the blow with a left high block.

Illus. 101. Now kick your opponent in the stomach with a right front kick.

Illus. 102. Strike him with a right forward fist to his stomach.

Practice these moves. Repeat this sequence ten times to each side.

Sequence 2

Illus. 103. Face your partner in a ready stance (far right). He stands in a left front stance.

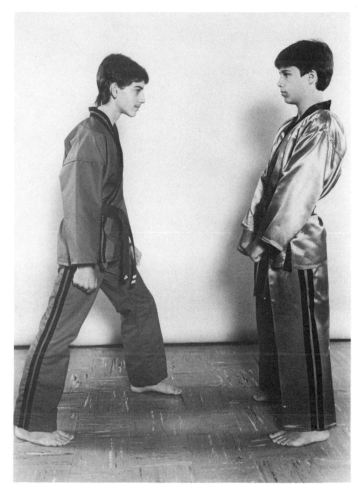

Illus. 104. He tries to punch you in the face with his right fist. Stop the blow with an outside middle block with your right arm.

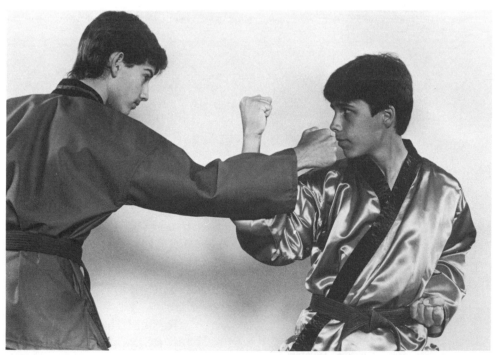

Illus. 105. Lift your right leg so your foot is at your left knee.

Illus. 106. Do a right side kick to his stomach.

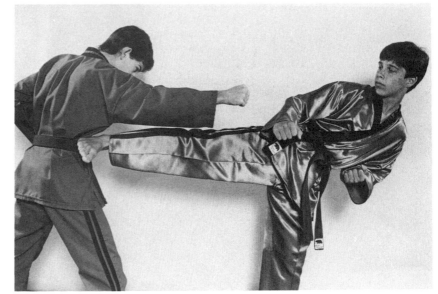

Illus. 107. Step towards your opponent and strike with a right back fist to his head.

Repeat the sequence ten times to each side.

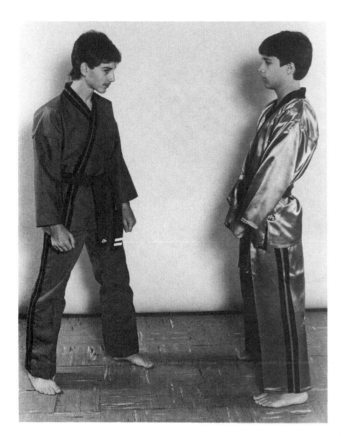

Sequence 3

Illus. 108. Face your partner in a ready stance (at right). He stands in a left front stance.

Illus. 109. He kicks with his right leg to your groin. Block with a left low block.

Illus. 110. Step forward into a right front stance while throwing a right forward fist to his chest.

Repeat the sequence ten times to each side.

Sequence 4

Illus. 111. Face your partner in a ready stance (at left). He stands in a left front stance.

Illus. 112. Stop your opponent's punch to your chest with an inside middle block with your left arm.

Illus. 113. Step into a right front stance and do a knife-hand strike to his neck with your right hand. Repeat the sequence ten times to each side.

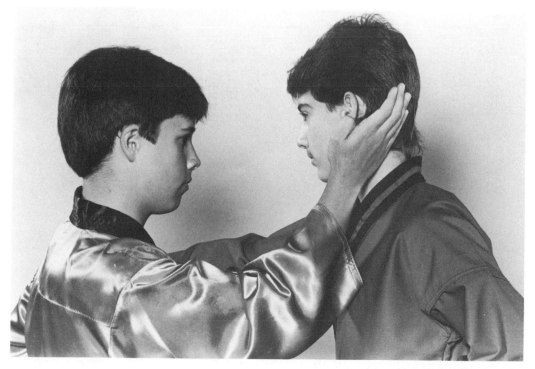

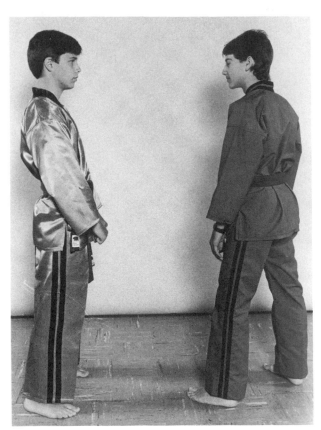

Sequence 5

Illus. 114. Face your partner in a ready stance (far left). He stands in a left ready stance.

Illus. 115. Block a front kick to your chest area with an inside middle block with your left arm as you move into a left front stance.

Illus. 116. Prepare to deliver a right roundhouse kick at your opponent's head.

Illus. 117. Raise your right leg with your foot cocked for the kick.

Illus. 118. Snap your lower leg for the kick.

Illus. 119. Complete the kick to his head.

Repeat the sequence ten times to each side.

Sequence 6

This one can be done by yourself.

Illus. 120. Begin from a right front stance.

Illus. 120.

Illus. 121. Swing your left leg forward and do a left front kick.

Illus. 122. Step forward again into a left front stance.

Illus. 121.

Illus. 122.

Illus. 123. Do a right side kick.

Illus. 124. Step forward, turn around, and finish with a left roundhouse kick.

Practice, repetition, and dedication should be your goals. If you stay with it, you will succeed in karate.

4
SPARRING

BOWING AND MEDITATION

Learning how to bow and meditate are as important to karate practice as correctly doing the basic techniques. Let's review the steps of bowing which you learned in Chapter 2:

1. Place your feet together and put your hands at your sides (Illus. 125).
2. Bend your body forward a little without moving legs or feet (Illus. 126).
3. Quickly return to a straight, standing position (Illus. 125).

Remember to keep your eyes on the person or object in front of you. Traditionally, you bow in the following situations:

1. When you enter or leave a karate class or school.
2. When you greet or leave the karate instructor.
3. At the beginning and end of all karate practice either with a partner or by yourself.
4. At the beginning and end of your meditation.

As you know by now, karate cannot be learned well if you don't pay attention. In other words, you won't be able to concentrate if your mind is full of other thoughts. If you meditate before every karate class or practice session, your mind will be as clear as it can be.

Illus. 125. The way to begin a bow.

Illus. 126. Bend at the waist.

Illus. 127. To meditate, first bow.

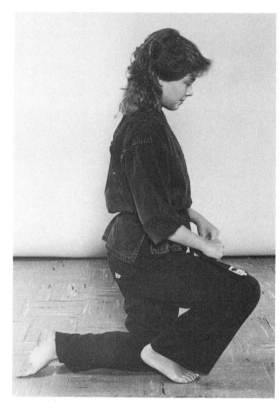

Illus. 128. Then lower your left knee to the floor.

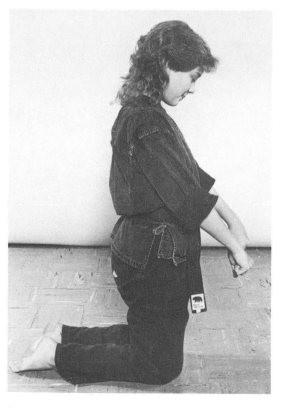

Illus. 129. Put your right knee on the floor.

Illus. 130. Lower your body on the back of your legs and sit on your heels.

Illus. 131. Rest your hands on your thighs and bend over a little.

Lower your head and close your eyes. Now start to clear your mind for karate class or practice. Think about your stances, or the motions for a front kick or punch.

Karate instructors usually ask for total silence and concentration from one to two minutes during meditation. It will help you to prepare for karate practice.

After you finish a class or practice, meditate again and think about what you have learned. Stand in a ready stance after you meditate. End the class or practice session with a bow.

Illus. 132. These students meditate before a class.

SELF-DEFENSE

Self-defense is an important part of karate. Blocks, kicks, strikes, and punches can help you defend yourself against a person of any size. If you get confused about when to fight back or defend yourself, you may become helpless or get hurt. As you gain experience in karate, you learn how to avoid fights and danger.

To learn self-defense, you practice prearranged movements. You spar, called ippon-kumite (ee-pon-koo-ma-ta), until you can defend yourself without much thought. Follow these three rules for self-defense:

1. Never use karate to start a fight.
2. Use karate as a defense if you are being attacked.
3. Strike an attacker only as hard as necessary for you to avoid injury. If one strike stops the attacker, don't use a second.

You will learn about prearranged sparring in this chapter. Be careful when you practice it. Never actually strike or kick anyone as you learn. There are many areas of the body to strike if someone attacks you. The best areas are: face, head, neck, chest, stomach, groin, knees, back, kidneys, and sides.

PREARRANGED SPARRING

You do prearranged, or planned, sparring (ippon-kumite) to practice self-defense. The student playing the attacker must first measure the length of his arm or leg from the defender's body. This is important so your partner never hits you. Stop your kick or punch about an inch from your partner's body. You can block using very light touching. But be careful.

In the following situations, first play the part of the defender. Later you can switch with your partner and be the attacker.

Illus. 133. This girl measures the distance to her teacher so she won't actually hit him when they spar.

Situation 1

Illus. 134. The attacker holds out his arm to measure the distance to your chest. Then he lowers it. At your command, the attacker throws a right punch to your chest.

Illus. 135. Move left into a horse stance and throw an outside middle block with your left arm to stop the punch. (Touch the attacker lightly with the block.)

Illus. 136. After the block, throw a left back fist to the attacker's head.

Illus. 137. Then move to a right front stance directly in front of the attacker. Aim a left front kick to his stomach.

Illus. 138. Return your foot to a left front stance as you move closer to the attacker. Throw a right punch to the attacker's chest.

Illus. 139. Finish your move with a left-hand punch to the head.

Situation 2

Illus. 140. The attacker holds out his arm to measure the distance to your chest. Then he throws a left-hand punch.

Illus. 141. Block the attack with a left inside block as you step back with your right leg into a left front stance.

Illus. 142. Quickly throw a right punch to his head.

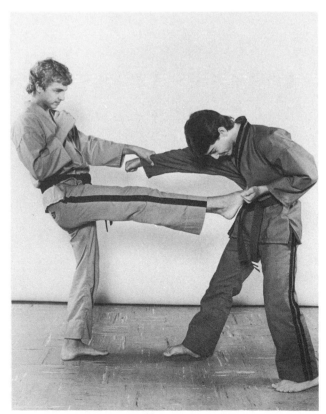

Illus. 143. Finish with a right front kick to his stomach.

Illus. 144.

Situation 3

Illus. 144. The attacker prepares and throws a right punch to your head. Block with a left rising block as you move into a left front stance.

Illus. 145. According to your distance from the attacker, you must decide either to step backwards with your left leg or forward into a front stance (Illus. 146).

In ippon-kumite, you judge the distance from your attacker and the speed of the attack to learn where to step.

Illus. 145.

Illus. 146.

Situation 4

Illus. 147. The attacker prepares and throws a right punch to your chest.

Illus. 148. Step into a left front stance. Block the attack with a left knife-hand block.

Illus. 149.

Illus. 150.

Illus. 149. Follow your block with a right knife-hand strike to the neck. You must note the speed and distance of the attack and decide to use your right knife hand in the same stance as the block or move into a right front stance (Illus. 150).

Illus. 151. Finish with a right front kick to the stomach.

Learn to be flexible and use many different blocks, punches, and kicks. So far, all of the attacks have been with the right hand and you have defended to your left. Practice with the attack from the left hand, which is the case in Situation 5.

Illus. 151.

Situation 5

Illus. 152. The attacker punches with his left hand.

Illus. 153. Turn to your right into a left front stance. Block with a left inside block.

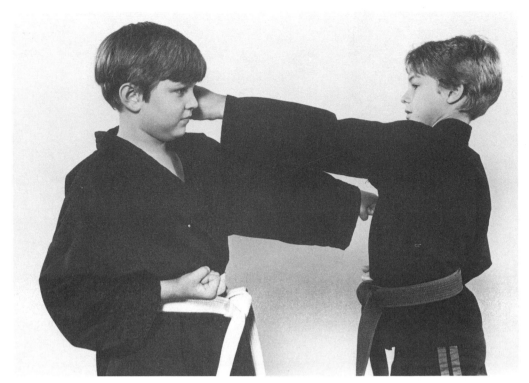

Illus. 154. Then strike with a left back fist to the face.

Illus. 155. Shift into a left front stance and do a right front kick to the stomach.

Illus. 156. Return to a front stance and punch the attacker in the chest with your left hand.

Illus. 157. Finish with a right punch.

Practice Situations 2, 3, and 4 with a left-hand attack. Reverse each defense by beginning the block with your left arm, and so on.

As you improve, the attacker can use kicks, back fists, or any other attack for you to defend. But make sure you know what the moves will be ahead of time. Try out several combinations of strikes, punches, and kicks. Don't mix techniques that won't work well together. For example, don't try to block a low kick with an outside middle block. The kick would be too low for the block to work.

Situation 6

Illus. 158. The attacker prepares and does a right front kick to the stomach. Return with a low block in a left front stance.

Illus. 159. Kick the attacker with a right front kick to the stomach.

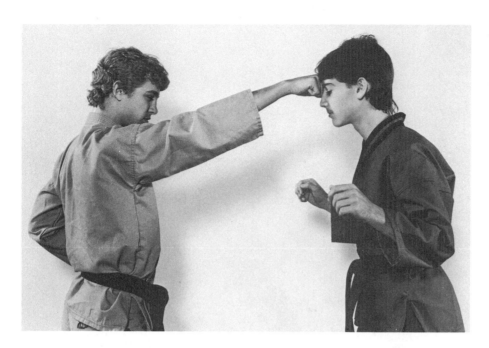

Illus. 160. Follow quickly with a right punch to the forehead.

Illus. 161. Repeat Situation 6 beginning with a left front kick. The defender counters with a low block from a right front stance.

Illus. 162. Return with a left front kick.

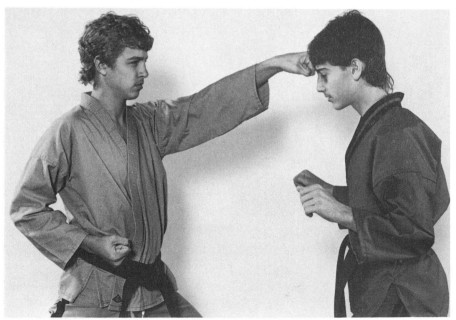

Illus. 163. Follow quickly with a left punch to the fore-head.

Practice all the situations until you feel comfortable with these self-defense skills.

FREE-STYLE SPARRING

In free-style sparring (jiyu-kumite), you don't use planned moves. You have no idea what your opponent will do. In sport karate (explained in Chapter 5), you win a point for each unblocked punch or kick to your opponent.

Kumite matches must be realistic. Situations change because you and your opponent both try to score points with kicks, punches, and strikes. Since each opponent is a moving target, your position and timing are important. You must learn to kick and punch where you think your opponent will be moving.

Illus. 164. After you kick your opponent . . .

Illus. 165. . . . quickly move close to him.

Situation 7

Illus. 166. Fake a left front kick.

Illus. 167. Then strike with a left back fist to the head.

Illus. 168. But suppose your back fist is blocked.

Illus. 169. Grab his arm and score with a right front kick since you are close to your opponent.

85

Since both fighters move freely in Situation 7, you may have to extend your back fist to score a point. Remember, your opponent can attack at the same time as you.

Illus. 170. Suppose your left back fist is blocked.

Illus. 171. Your opponent throws a right punch to your stomach and scores a point. Points can be scored by either opponent during the two- or three-minute match.

Use many different punches and kicks while sparring. The more strikes and kicks you use, the greater your chances to score a point. Look at Situation 8.

Situation 8

Illus. 172. Close the distance between you and your opponent by taking a step forward with your left foot. Fake a left back fist to the head.

Illus. 173. Follow with a fast roundhouse kick with your right leg. But your opponent blocks it with his left arm.

Illus. 174. Do a left front kick. He blocks it with his right arm.

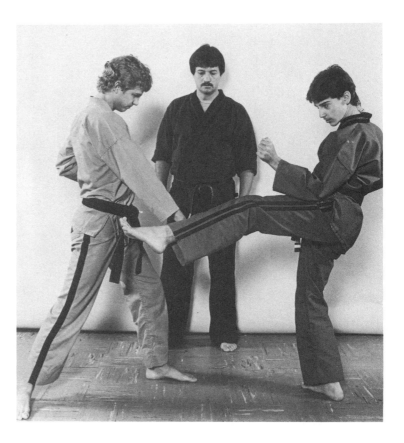

Illus. 175. Throw a right punch to the chest to score.

You can score points after blocking an attack. After you block, try to score a point as soon as you can. Look at the next situation.

Situation 9

Illus. 176. Block your opponent's right front kick with a left low block.

Illus. 177. Then throw a right punch to the chest for the score.

Illus. 178. Block a left back fist with a left inside block.

Illus. 179. Then block a low roundhouse kick with a right low block.

Illus. 180. Strike with a right front kick to the stomach to score.

Situation 11

Illus. 181. Your opponent does a right side kick to your upper body. Block with an outside center block with your left arm.

Illus. 182. Counter with a right roundhouse kick to the head to score.

Situation 12

Illus. 183. Do a front kick with your right leg. But your opponent blocks it with a left low block.

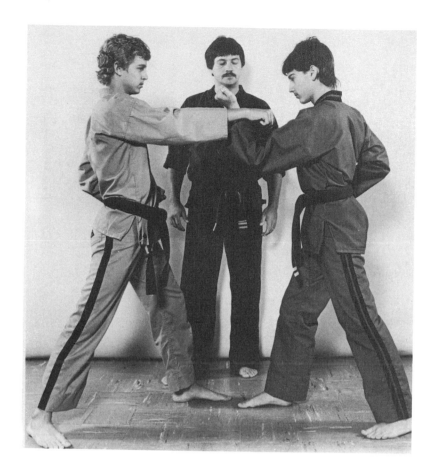

Illus. 184. He throws a right punch to your chest, which you block with a left middle block.

Illus. 185. Your opponent scores with a left side kick to the chest.

Summary

You can use many karate skills in free-style sparring. Use blocks as a defense and then strike with punches and kicks to score. Follow these rules when you spar:

1. You score a point when you do a kick or punch that is not blocked.
2. The areas to aim for are: head, face, upper body, stomach, and groin. Strikes to the kidneys, arms, shoulders, or legs are not counted as points.
3. Strikes to the lower back and kidneys are not allowed in most karate matches.
4. Strike near the target. *Body contact is not allowed*. Stop kicks and punches an

Illus. 186. The boy at left scores a point with an unblocked punch to the stomach.

inch from your opponent's body. Careless or wild movements can seriously hurt someone.
5. Wear protective equipment (mouthpiece, headgear, cup athletic supporter for boys, padded gloves for hands and feet).
6. Bow at the beginning and end of each match and after a point is scored. Bow to the judge and your opponent.

Illus. 187. **Never strike the lower back or kidneys. The boy at far left should aim a punch to his opponent's head.**

Illus. 188. **Strike near the target, but do not make contact.**

Illus. 189. Bow to the instructor at the beginning and end of each match.

Illus. 190. Then bow to your opponent.

96

5

KATAS AND COMPETITIONS

Karate, as mentioned before, was first practiced as an art in the Orient. Some people believe that it was developed long ago by men watching animals fight. Although many karate kicks and punches look like animal movements, the true beginning of karate is unknown.

The movements of karate are beautiful and graceful. As you learn the art of these movements, you may grow to appreciate their beauty. Karate is not just an activity. It can help you to improve everything in your life.

Many instructors teach only physical skills of karate. Meditation and the beauty of karate may be completely overlooked. On the other hand, there are instructors who just teach karate as an art form. They may not encourage you to practice for tournaments and sport karate. To get the most from karate, you should be able to practice the beautiful movements as you compete in the sport.

The best example of the art of karate is the kata (ka-tuh).

KATAS

In karate, katas are planned moves that look like ballet or dance. You can use katas to practice your blocks, kicks, strikes, and punches in a graceful pattern of movements.

You practice katas by yourself. Imagine that you are being attacked. Throw punches and kicks in a planned order. Most advanced katas look like the movements of a cat, snake, tiger, and other animals. They also look like letters of the alphabet, such as H, T, K, or a plus sign (+).

All katas have a name or number. Many instructors use katas that were developed by the great karate masters. Some katas are changed by instructors or new ones are created to help their students.

Think of a kata as a dance. Practice each step in order. As you improve your skills, you can learn katas that are more difficult. Katas are beautiful to do or watch.

The kata described here is for begin-

Illus. 191. This girl practices kata movements by herself.

ners, and it is called Sheno (she-no). If you were to watch the movement from above, it would look like a plus sign (+).

As you do the kata, the way you breathe is very important. To breathe correctly, keep a lot of air in your lungs. Take a deep breath before you do a block, kick, or strike. Exhale as you do the movement.

To increase your strength, breathe out heavily when doing the final action in a series. Shout a loud "ee-ay" while breathing out. Your power and confidence should improve. But do it only in the last move in a series.

Illus. 192. Some of the movements look like a dance.

Illus. 193. Exhale as you do a punch, kick, or block.

Sheno Kata

Illus. 194. Bow.

Illus. 195. Breathe in as you bend your left leg and cross your arms in front of you.

Illus. 194.

Illus. 195.

Illus. 196. Breathe out and stand in a ready stance.

Illus. 197. Step forward into a left front stance and do a left low block.

Illus. 196.

Illus. 197.

101

Illus. 198.

Illus. 199.

Illus. 198. Do a right front kick.

Illus. 199. Return to a left front stance.

Illus. 200.

Illus. 201.

Illus. 200. Punch at chest level with your right fist.

Illus. 201. Follow with a left punch.

Illus. 202. Turn your head to your left.

Illus. 203. Turn your body to your far left into a left forward stance and do a rising block with your left arm.

Illus. 204. Do a front kick with your right foot at stomach level and return your foot to the floor.

Illus. 205. Throw a right punch.

Illus. 202.

Illus. 203.

Illus. 204.

Illus. 205.

Illus. 206.

Illus. 207.

Illus. 208.

Illus. 206. Follow with a left punch.

Illus. 207. Pivot on your left leg, turning your right leg and body 180° around to your right side into a right front stance (Illus. 208).

Illus. 208. At the same time, do an inside middle block with your right arm.

Illus. 209.

Illus. 210.

Illus. 211.

Illus. 209. Do a left front kick to the stomach area.

Illus. 210. Return your foot and throw a left punch to the head area.

Illus. 211. Follow with a right punch to the lower body area. (Shout "ee-ay" when you do this punch.)

Illus. 212.

Illus. 213.

Illus. 214.

Illus. 212 Turn your right leg 90° to your right into a right forward stance.

Illus. 213. At the same time, do an inside middle block with your right arm.

Illus. 214. Without moving either foot, do an inside middle block with your left arm.

Illus. 215.

Illus. 216.

Illus. 217.

Illus. 215. Hold your left fist in front with your right fist at your hip.

Illus. 216. Punch to the chest area with your right fist.

Illus. 217. Follow with a left punch.

Illus. 218. Finish by lifting your right leg and spin completely around to the left to your original position (Illus. 218–Illus. 222).

Illus. 218.

Illus. 219.

Illus. 220.

Illus. 221.

Illus. 222.

Illus. 223.

Illus. 224.

Illus. 225.

Illus. 222. Breathe in and cross your arms in front of you.

Illus. 223. Breathe out and lower your arms and right leg.

Illus. 224. Close your stance.

Illus. 225. Bow.

In the Sheno kata, you can practice some of the basic punches and blocks. You do front kicks with both legs. You also learn the proper method of moving from one stance to another.

Try to improve your form and power as you do this kata. Take your time and go slowly. Do not increase your speed unless you can do it evenly.

Katas are considered by many instructors to be a large part of karate. They are also used to grade rank. The higher the rank, the faster and stronger the kata.

KARATE COMPETITIONS

Karate is a very popular sport. Many tournaments are held throughout the United States and the entire world. If you can travel, you could enter a tournament every week.

In a tournament, you can enter three or four events, according to your rank. The events include kata, self-defense, and kumite. You can compete with opponents of the same rank. Rank divisions include white belt (beginner), green belt (intermediate), brown belt (advanced), and black belt (expert). The white-belt division may also include yellow and orange belts. The green division may also include blue belts.

Illus. 226. These students compete in a karate tournament.

Three to five judges will watch you do a kata. Each judge scores your kata on a scale from one to ten. The highest average score wins. You could win trophies in first, second, or third places in each division. Judges are black belts and rate you according to form, speed, and difficulty of your kata.

In self-defense, you may compete in a team or group. Usually, three to five students pretend to be attacked. Judges rate the group according to form, speed, and creativity. A group of self-defense students is usually from the same karate school.

In kumite, you are divided by rank and weight. Weight divisions are usually heavy and light. In a kumite match, you spar for two or three minutes. You try to kick or punch your opponent without being blocked. When this happens you score one point. The player who scores the first three points, or

Illus. 227. This boy gets instruction with his class on self-defense.

Illus. 228. The boy at right scores a point with a kick to his opponent's stomach.

who has the most points at the end, wins the match. In case of a tie, you continue until the next score. You continue the kumite matches until there are first-, second-, and third-place winners.

Illus. 228a. A trophy won in a karate competition makes any student proud.

6
ADVANCED TECHNIQUES

Once you learn the basic punches, kicks, and blocks described in Chapter 3, you can begin learning some advanced techniques. But don't think you can stop practicing the basic moves. Even karate experts continue to use them all the time. No matter how advanced you become, you will use the basic moves the most. Practice them every day. The advanced techniques give you the chance to add to your karate skills.

ADVANCED KICKS

Crescent Kick

Do the crescent kick with your front leg in a front stance. You can strike with this kick, but many people find it more useful for blocking. Follow these steps for a left crescent kick:

Illus. 229. Stand in a left front stance. As your opponent throws a right punch, kick your left leg up and make contact with his arm.

Illus. 230. Push the arm over to the left to block the punch with the left side of your foot. Then return your foot to a left front stance.

Spin Kick

Follow these steps to do a right spin kick:

Illus. 231. Stand in a left front stance. With your left leg, step across to your right side to start the spin of your body.

Illus. 232. At the same moment, lift your right leg, which should be bent at the knee.

Illus. 233. Spin around, then straighten your leg to make contact with your target. Use the heel and right edge of your foot.

Fake Front Roundhouse Kick

Use the fake front roundhouse kick in self-defense or kumite. Follow these steps to do this kick with your right foot:

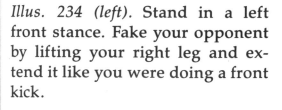

Illus. 234 (left). **Stand in a left front stance. Fake your opponent by lifting your right leg and extend it like you were doing a front kick.**

Illus. 235 (right). Just before you complete the kick, twist your right leg so it is parallel to the floor.

Illus. 236 (left). **Finish with a roundhouse kick to your opponent's head. Once you master this kick, it is most difficult to block.**

Hook Kick

This kick is similar to the fake front roundhouse kick. Your opponent will think you are doing a front kick. Follow these steps to do a hook kick with your right leg:

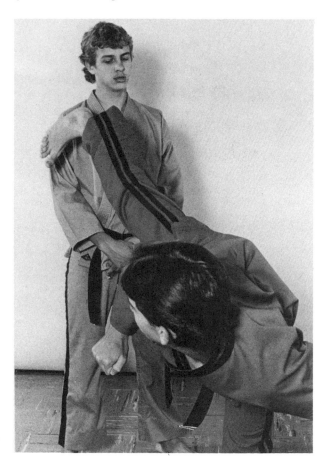

Illus. 237. Aim a right front kick at your opponent. Just as your right leg is blocked, rotate it in a circle to the left.

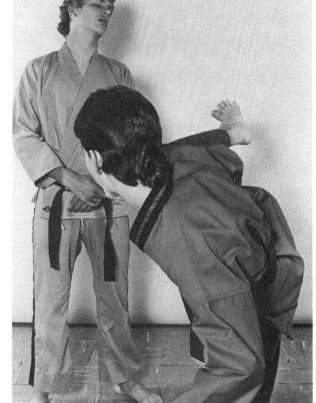

Illus. 238. Continue to bring your right foot around and "hook" your opponent's head with the right edge of your foot.

ADVANCED STRIKES

Palm-Heel Strike

Use the palm-heel strike as a punch. Follow these steps for a strike with your right hand from any stance:

Illus. 239. Hold your right hand up, palm facing your opponent. Bend your fingers slightly.

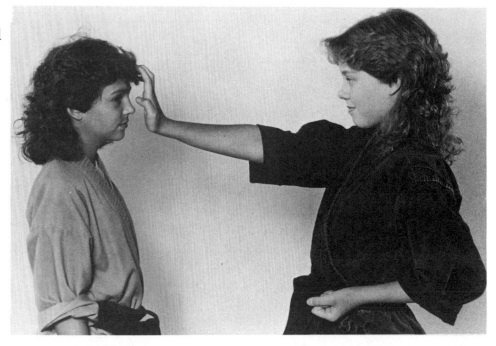

Illus. 240. Push your hand forward and lock your elbow. Aim for your opponent's nose or upper head with the heel of your palm.

Do not strike the mouth area. Your opponent's teeth could hurt your hand if you were to hit them.

Ridge-Hand Strike

Use the ridge hand to strike the upper head or neck area. You can also use this move to block. Follow these steps for a right ridge-hand strike:

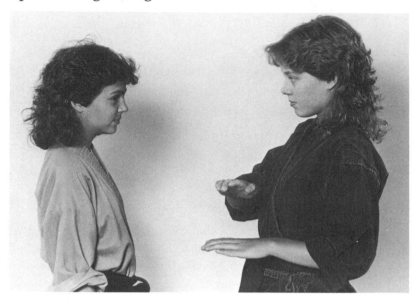

Illus. 241. Hold your right hand in front, palm down. Bend your thumb towards your palm. Bend your fingertips slightly.

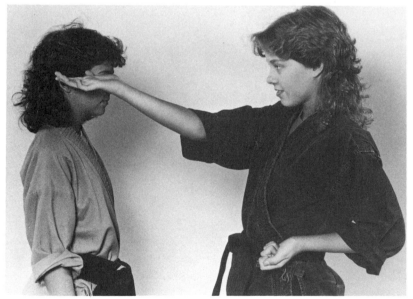

Illus. 242. Bend your wrist to form an upside-down "L" with your arm. Before you strike, pull your right hand in close to the left side of your body. Snap your hand outward at your target.

Illus. 243. The position of the hand for a ridge-hand strike.

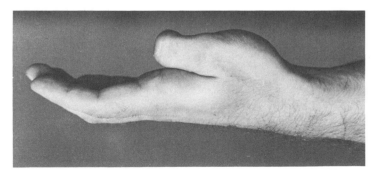

Knee Strike

Your knee can be used to strike your opponent. Follow these steps to do a right knee strike:

Illus. 244. From a front stance, your opponent throws a right punch. Block with an outside middle block.

Illus. 245. (above) Then grab your opponent's right shoulder.

Illus. 246. (left) Pull forward and bend your right knee, striking the chest.

ADVANCED BLOCKS

X-Block

This is called the X-block because you cross your arms in an "X" when you do it. Follow these steps for the X-block:

Illus. 247. Stand in a left front stance with your arms in front of your chest.

Illus. 248. As your opponent kicks her right leg, lower your arms and cross them in front to block it.

The X-block can also be used to block a hammer strike to your head. You cross your arms and raise them to block your opponent's arm. In this case, a rising block is usually the best defense.

Leg Sweep

Follow these steps for a leg sweep. Use this move to knock your opponent to the ground:

Illus. 249. From a left front stance, your opponent attacks with a punch. After you block the punch, step to your left side, and place your right leg behind your opponent's front leg.

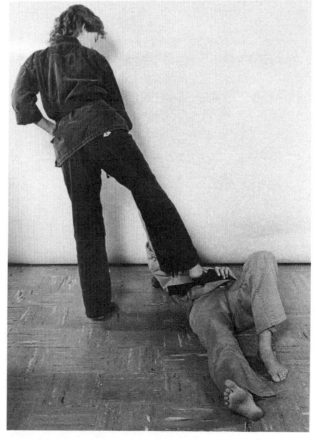

Illus. 250. Sweep rearwards with your leg, knocking your opponent to the ground.

Only if it is necessary, strike your opponent with a low front kick.

ADVICE TO PARENTS

Children have many interests at various stages in their development. Many want to learn to play musical instruments, such as guitar or piano. Frequently, children participate in numerous sports, such as football, basketball, tennis, ice skating, and track and field. With the availability of movies and television programs about karate, young children of today show interest in learning it. Many children even imitate karate actors while at play.

Once your child has expressed interest in learning karate, it is important for you to provide support and guidance, whether instruction is learned in a karate class or from a book. As with any new study, the novelty will wear off soon, especially with children. Be aware that not all children have the motivation or desire to continue with karate, but with proper guidance this problem can be avoided.

Before investing a lot of money in a karate class for your child, use this book as an introduction to it. Follow the directions closely with your child. By showing encouragement and giving assistance, your child's interest can grow. Reinforce his

Illus. 251. It is best to get personal attention from a good instructor.

or her understanding about karate. In no time, you may see your child become self-motivated. If you are physically able, take up karate with your child, especially in the beginning stages. Carefully review each chapter of this book before you continue.

Children enjoy wearing a belt that shows their particular rank in karate. The beginning students wear a white belt, which is the eighth level. The karate techniques introduced in this book will take the student to the seventh and sixth levels of beginning study. The seventh level is a yellow belt and the sixth level is orange. Most students find these levels the most difficult because of the newness of learning karate.

After six months of continuous practice, enter your child in a karate school which has a special class for children and an instructor who will give them individual attention.

At this time, most children should be ready for intermediate levels, five and four. Level five is a green belt and level four is a blue belt. The average student who practices regularly can reach these ranks within another six months to one year. From blue belt, the student will enter the ranks of a brown belt—level three, level two, and then level one. All three levels of a brown belt require a total of twelve to eighteen months of study beyond a blue belt in most cases. After the first level of brown is achieved, it takes about one year to become a Shodan or first-degree black belt, which is considered expert status. Black belt degrees range from first degree to tenth degree. Very few karate practitioners achieve past second degree, unless their entire life is devoted to karate.

Karate has different systems and styles, although many are quite similar. Most styles are from Japan, Okinawa, China, and Korea. The style introduced in this book is from Japan and is called Shito-ryu (shee-toe-ru). It is most similar to other Japanese styles such as Shotokan (show-toe-kon) and Goju-ryu (go-jew-ru).

Index